Going to College

Building Bridges Series

Gate
HOUSE

Building Bridges Series: Going to College
Text by Catherine White
Illustrations by Marta Kwasniewska
Copyright © Gatehouse Media Limited 2017

First published and distributed in 2017 by Gatehouse Media Limited

ISBN: 978-1-84231-173-8

British Library Cataloguing-in-Publication Data:
A catalogue record for this book is available from the British Library

As a child, in his home country,
Jamal went to school.
He was a good student.
His best subject was maths.
He also liked to draw.

As a child, Jamal liked to watch
the men at work on building sites.
He watched the men build new homes.
He watched the men build new offices.
He watched them build roads.
He watched them build a bridge
across the river.

As a child, Jamal liked bridges.
He liked to draw pictures of bridges.
He liked to make bridges
and play with them with his friends.
He made bridges out of sticks and wood.
He made bridges out of stones and sand.

Jamal and his friends played with toy cars
and toy boats.
The toy cars drove over the bridge.
The toy boats sailed under the bridge.

Jamal wanted to learn how to build
real bridges.

He said, "When I leave school,
I will go to university.
I will study engineering.
I will learn how to build bridges."

But then the war started
and Jamal had to leave his home country.
Now Jamal is in England.

Jamal wants to study.

He wants to go to university.

He wants to be an engineer.

He wants to be a civil engineer.

Jamal says, "One day, I will build a bridge."

Jamal enrols at his local college.

First, he needs to learn English.

Then he needs to sit exams in maths.

He needs to sit exams in physics.

He wants to study design and technology, too.

"I must get good grades
so I can go to university," says Jamal.
"I must get good grades
so I can become an engineer."

"One day, I will build a bridge!"

If you have enjoyed this book, why not try another title in the *Building Bridges Series:*

Gatehouse Books®

Gatehouse Books are written for older teenagers and adults who are developing their basic reading and writing or English language skills.

The format of our books is clear and uncluttered.
The language is familiar and the text is often line-broken, so that each line ends at a natural pause.

Gatehouse Books are widely used within Adult Basic Education throughout the English speaking world.
They are also a valuable resource within the Prison Education Service and Probation Services, Social Services and secondary schools - in both basic skills and ESOL teaching.

Catalogue available

Gatehouse Media Limited
PO Box 965
Warrington
WA4 9DE

Tel/Fax: 01925 267778
E-mail: info@gatehousebooks.com
Website: www.gatehousebooks.com